S
U
D
D
E
N
L
Y

D
E

C

I

DUO

US

Suddenly Deciduous
by Dee Slavutin

Finishing Line Press
Georgetown, Kentucky

Suddenly Deciduous

For Lydia, who showed me deciduous contains "duo" and "us"

For Aaron, who taught me how to do a page-break in word

For Lee, who is still my husband and still takes out the garbage

Copyright © 2026 by Dee Slavutin
ISBN 979-8-89990-302-1 First Edition
All rights reserved under International and Pan-American Copyright Conventions. No part of this book may be reproduced in any manner whatsoever without written permission from the publisher, except in the case of brief quotations embodied in critical articles and reviews.

ACKNOWLEDGMENTS

Wingspan: search for Food 2013
shadow lane press
Things
Not Enough
Long Island Sounds 2018
Yes, But Why Now
Ruth Weiss Foundation Haiku Contest 2024 finalist
Aging in Haiku
All the Women Came and Sang
Wyld Syde Press, 2025
2:30AM
CAMOUFLAGE
THE MOSQUITO BITE
POLYESTER NEVER DIES
TODAY, I'LL STAY STILL
UTERINE TRAVELER

Publisher: Leah Huete de Maines
Editor: Christen Kincaid
Cover Art: Lydia Slavutin
Author Photo: Lydia Slavutin
Cover Design: Elizabeth Maines McCleavy and Lydia Slavutin

Order online: www.finishinglinepress.com
also available on amazon.com

Author inquiries and mail orders:
Finishing Line Press
PO Box 1626
Georgetown, Kentucky 40324
USA

Contents

Section One—Aging
- Suddenly Deciduous ... 1
- The Martini Olive ... 2
- Overnight Flight ... 3
- Voice Over ... 4
- Yes, But Why Now? ... 5
- Aging Tree ... 6
- The Captain's Scarlet ... 7
- Aging in Haiku ... 8
- Across the Street ... 9
- The Patch ... 10
- Retired ... 11
- Stop Looking for Yesterday ... 12
- Left Here ... 13
- Old Love ... 14
- Not Enough ... 15
- The Wiser Condiment ... 16
- Will There be Milk Tomorrow? ... 17
- Do You Remember me? ... 18
- We Did ... 19
- Our Quiet Breath ... 20
- "I Love You Too Sweetheart" ... 21
- Geezer/Geyser ... 22
- August Say Goodbye ... 23
- A Man with a Bouquet ... 24
- A Man who Makes Money ... 25
- Some Things We're Forgetting ... 26

Section Two—Nuclear Family
- She Cannot Hear Me ... 29
- Ink-Blot Memories of My Mother ... 30
- Gloria's Last Crossword Puzzle ... 31
- My Mother Always Fed the Birds ... 32
- My Mother's Magnifying Mirror ... 33
- Momma Can't Answer ... 34
- She Doesn't Even Know ... 35
- Rush ... 36
- Who's your Daddy? ... 37
- 168th and Broadway ... 38
- Double Doors ... 39

    For my son 40
    Make Believe 41
    Polyester Never Dies 42

Section Three—Reflections
    Stingy 45
    His Cart 46
    On My Walk 47
    Do Not Do 48
    Things 49
    Evening Fire 50
    At Quail Hill Farm 51
    Moss 52
    Just Pretendin' 53
    Three Clocks 54
    Let's Schmooz 55
    His Grandpa's Tree 56
    A Gift from Bob 57
    The Nurse 58
    Bus Route out my Window during Covid 59
    No Ordinary Lemon 60
    My Prayer 61
    Zen in Hand… Haiku Gusts 62
    Four Haiku about Birds 64
    Sea Between us 65

Section Four—Animals Of Any Kind
    Migration 69
    In the beak of Prayer 70
    In my Pool 71
    Send his Body Home 72
    Today I'll Stay Still 73
    The Steer 74
    A Stallion in my Dream 75
    I Thought I had a bad night 76
    Swansong 77
    Hoarder 78
    Uterine Traveler 79
    Crabgrass 80
    Camouflage 81
    The Mosquito Bite 82
    Please Come Out 83
    2:32 AM 84

Introduction

Where this Writer Goes

I step into a birthplace called darktronomy.
No horizontal, no vertical, no entry point.
Only inside.
Untethered, I roam with the invisible new moon.
Blackness lights my way.
Obsidian vapors hurdle me beyond the already told,
escort me to a blank white page
where I aim to collide with you.
Join me on my weightless journey,
my words orbit just for you.
They are not distant.
I've left them here for you to touch.

SECTION ONE

AGING

Suddenly Deciduous

Nothing left on this tree.
I am woody in dry soil.
My December howl deepens.
After this somnolent shedding,
I will become a hundred-year-old table
stained with rings of late-night lonely beers.

The Martini Olive

Was it a lifetime ago I rolled it in my mouth
let it sit inside my cheek, careful not to pierce the skin,
play cat and mouse with the fattened fruit?
The olive was round and whole,
my mouth a moist galaxy.

Reluctant to spit it out,
my teeth crunch the ruts,
aging gums and tongue on safari
for green reminiscent shards.

I said "no" to the one with one blue eye,
 "no" to the one with freckles.
My vanilla silk wedding dress, simple,
knee-length, a bodice of antique lace.

I return the olive to its bath,
comforting clunk, cool spray on my cheek.
The clear gin magnifies
stingy love I gave my mother,
shame of my father's jail time,
jealousy of G-d who stole my husband's devotion.

Glass tilted, courage summoned,
I invite myself to suck the flesh,
as if I could whittle these regrets,
remand the remnants to a foreign galaxy,
spit out the rutted pit.

There's no one here to tell me how old I am.

Overnight Flight

Say goodnight to the day,
good evening to the night,
Paris morning awaits.

Pre-dawn, Atlantic crossed,
the taxi driver smokes his Gauloises.
 AM pick-ups need nicotine.
I roll down my window,
smoke mingles with morning mist,
hovers seductively.

Mustached sweepers in the dawn
caress centuries-old cobblestones.
The rhythmic purr of bristle brooms
lingers like a stroke on my thigh.

It takes a continent, vintage Europe,
to prompt these old bones.
A baguette, espresso,
of course, a bicycle,
a lover,
even a cigarette.

Someone with a match
will light a flame,
lay his jacket over a puddle for me.

Voice Over

I invite the ghosts to show their faces,
to replay scenes of haunted memories
to contradict them.

The one I loved, but not enough.
Pretending to be someone else,
I stepped over his drugged body.

A teenager, caught in a plot to steal,
my mouth still fills with dead-white fear.

Father, recycling my childhood shame,
serving time in his seventies.

Our car-less driveway, blank as a void check.
Other mothers drove us to the movies,
wore red lipstick, reminded us of pick-up time.

"So What!"

Run the credits, I made them stars.
The curled celluloid is now clipped on the floor.

Time to stop following my life like a dog its master.
I'm the director. This is my voice-over.

Yes, But Why Now?

Yes,
the osprey builds her nest,
a doe teaches silence in the woods,
the sun slants up the East.

But,
observe the browning of edges,
the pallor of a tired moth,
a beetle on its back.

Why,
does the daylily die,
the hummingbird depart,
you forget me?

Now,
as memory greys,
let the mosquito warm itself
in the tunnel of my last breath.

Aging Tree

In Winter, the moonbeams you lure
reveal gnarled roots, contorted limbs.
Yet, you stand naked without shame.
I see your stature.

In Spring, you lose a limb in heavy rain;
burdened with mud, pink buds drown.
Thereafter, you live with partial death.
I see your wholeness.

In Summer, you sway off losses.
The rustle of your green crown
claims your share of eternity.
I see your majesty.

In Fall, your flirtations fade.
You drop your guard,
but preserve the bare essentials.
I see your character.

I am witness to the secrets of your proud turnings,
how the seasons trained you.

A yellow-eyed bird sleeps in your hollow.
In my mirror, I want to own my wintering.

The Captain's Scarlet

The Hudson River's waves slap the hull.
A grey-bearded captain kisses the sky.
From shore I watch dawn burnish his day.
He razor-cuts the tide in two,
moors under the moon's arc,
commands the mist to disappear.

I dropped anchor for dry land,
live in rarely shaken snow globe.
Perfect translucent confetti storms
are no match for the breathing sea.

The ship's iron hull, the sun's scarlet,
wanderlust pulls me.
Fluid horizons are too intangible.

At dusk, the wake's whipped foam
churns my last chance.
Hoist me from my colorless life,
bind me to your dawn, your dusk.
I will paint my lips scarlet.
Kiss me the way you kissed the sky.

Aging in Haiku

3 Takes off her diaper
Fingers tie new shoelaces
Shares her toys with friends

13 Cherry breast buds bud
Something red between her legs
Girlhood bliss kiss

23 Her breasts command him
The mirror silver streams them
Touches womanhood

33 Flowing milk in breasts
Suckling children ignite love
Motherhood is born

43 Stretch-t-back sports bra
Homework, pay bills, walk dog, cook
Wide smiles in sleep

53 Topless on French beach
Marriage bed erupts again
Black lingerie heaped

63 Her breasts are removed
Bed, still, is always quiet
Questions not answered

73 Sunbathe on nude beach
Loud bed is never quiet
Answers come on wings

83 Now, there is no their
Closes her eyes to see him
No one to hold her

93 Puts on her diaper
Fingers can't tie shoelaces
You can have her toys

Across the Street

Up early, out of habit when caffeine fueled my career,
I see into their kitchen and dining room.
Living in a New York City high-rise,
we don't call this spying.

In the dark, already in his white-collar shirt,
he stirs dawn's arrival, as I still do,
with a coffee spoon. His briskly, mine slowly.
He's gone completely bald in seven years.

His girls now brush their curly hair
straight back into ponytails.
Their bopping around the dining table,
slowed to teenage moping.
Coloring books traded for computers.

He leaves while his children are still dreaming.
So did I. I still question if
I sewed enough costumes,
baked enough brownies,
attended enough soccer games?
Our Thanksgiving is half empty sometimes.

At twilight, my coffee replaced with a cabernet,
I see Mom in the kitchen, the girls set the table.
They wait for him, then eat together.
In my now empty home, I raise my glass,
a toast to family.

The Patch

The shame of it in Summer!
I quickly wrapped my beach towel
to conceal protruding adolescence.
Now, looking down, I wonder
where the patch has gone,
where all the tufts have gone?

I miss the simian swirls
in the forests under my arms.
The lady-Schick rusts in the shower,
my legs need no lather.

My mink-thick brows arched
over bedroom eyes,
said "shut the door."
Now, almost none to pluck,
the bedroom needs no lock.

What good are goose bumps?
No hairs to stand on end,
can't jump into your arms,
yell "save me!"

A chin hair, wire-stiff, scuzzy,
angelic peach fuzz, a memory.
The mirror startles, my shoulders shrug.
Has it all gone down the drain?

In summer I cast aside the beach towel.
There is nothing left to hide!

Retired

Jan 2,
the world has gone back to work.
I have not.
I picked kale in the winter freeze,
bought paint for the kitchen project,
watered the plants,
scoured mildew from the shower,
pulled hairs from the vacuum.

I sit in front of the fire,
watch the disintegration of a tree.
Mine to cut down
to make room for the pool.
Alive now dead.

I recorded my face on my Iphone.
It is my face,
yet, I don't recognize my life.

Stop Looking for Yesterday

When fallen pine needles matted into auburn bedding,
the sharpness, now woven, seemed soft enough.
We learned how to sleep in the center of the silent carpet.
Upon waking we ate fall fruit, buried the pits,
prayed for resurrection of young lovers' might.

Partisans in the mad search for yesterday,
to thrust us back into each other's arms,
we slept in the belly of a canoe at the bay's shoreline,
on the iced side of a snow-hewn mountain,
on the cliff claimed by wolves in winter.

Shivering, we held hands,
discovered the way home
to our kitchen table,
the place of our aging intimacy.
Coffee, conversation,
your striped-blue shirt,
the sight of the back of your neck.

Left Here

Even our bone marrow was married.
A continuous certainty curled at the foot of our bed.
Your key in the door told the world to wait outside.

We circled into our center.
Everything was round, seamless,
spun by a sacred hand.
Your listening, quiet as daybreak.

Now, the tumbler is soundless.
No more sitting, leaning on an elbow
while coffee steams sense from dreams.

A lonely curlicue, circling from a single cup
shrouds the divinity of our pairing.
I want to sit again with you,
breathe the air you breathed.

Old Love

Archaeologists, scouring for true love's origin,
will find traces of our peppermint tea.
Coffee cups, cereal bowls hold a half-century
of round conversations on gluey spaghetti nights.

A couple ambles down the street.
Intrigued by the angle of her hip scraping his leg,
extending a rub, like jazz notes,
I'm sure they caress amid sips of wine,
 then sleep entwined like we used to.

Sometimes romance gets traded-in,
an identity walks away.
Swaying hips lose their swagger,
life gets less curvy.

Filled with grace, poured with concrete strength,
our urns have no jagged edges, no weapons.
The diggers will discover us in a love song.

Not Enough

Because the wall is not enough, we hang a picture.
Because the picture is not enough, we add a frame.
Because the frame is not enough, we direct a beam of light.
The light is not enough, we add an admirer.
One admirer is not enough, we get married.
Marriage is not enough, we have children.
There we all are, in the picture.

The Wiser Condiment

In dreams she guzzles an old lover,
then, with damp curls,
kissing risk in the face,
gallops off to ride another horse.

Now, devotion, a wiser condiment,
pollinates enduring love.
Night pines eavesdrop on sultry conversation
for hints of their agreed-upon elixir.

Though crystalized honey doesn't drizzle,
evergreen romance soothes them to sleep.
Her cheek in his palm.
His face, only his face.
The buzz round her glows.

Will There be Milk Tomorrow?

Yes, of course, he's coming home.
He only went for milk.
And you across the street,
on the 13th floor eating dinner,
do not care if he does or doesn't.
When he returns with whole instead of 2%
 I rejoice for the added fat he brings.
He has come home to me with a quart of milk.

Do You Remember me?

Would he notice
if the bills are unpaid
the garbage is full
dishes crust the sink,
the plants are dead?

None of this is true.
I am a perfect wife,
but I am thirsty.
My amorous days
blurred in a dusty picture.

The mink bustier,
black velvet dress,
strutting in fishnet
at the bedroom door.
No need to beckon.

Flannel sweats,
not lace
now embrace my thighs.

I beckon for his arms
to reach the tomato sauce
on the top shelf.

We Did

We know which floorboards creak,
the ones that rub against each other.
Nails too far apart, we walk around them.

Though felled, sawed, laid,
a tree's age-circles still yearn.
Wood wants continuous humidity,
even when pressure-treated.

There are methods devised to silence squeaks.
With surplus nails we laid a plush carpet
up against our tattooed temperaments,
to make sure we never undo the I do that we did.

Our Quiet Breath

Back then
I could no longer hear my own voice.
Its laconic echo revealed a lonely universe
lodged in black granite without a shuttle.

Somehow, I traveled to you.
Now, flooded in a wordless world,
as though Noah intended
love's silence to drench every pair,
we elope daily in the quiet pendulum
of each other's breath.

Let's not allow our breath to fade.
With you, there's no need to speak.

"I Love You Too Sweetheart"

It used to be I could only say
"love you."
Pronoun-less, noncommittal,
even though we were married.

Then, the androgenous merger of pronouns,
"we love you."

Now, I have no resistance.
"I love you too sweetheart."

We start our day with coffee,
end it with a kiss.
The hours in between,
articulate with speechless knowing.

We're both still here:
Cause enough to be in love.
Cause enough to say it.

Geezer/Geyser

"All hot spring activity,
is caused by surface water
… seeping down through the ground
until it meets rock heated by magma."

"How was dinner?" his Mrs. asked.
The waitress was delicious
mused the grey geezer.
He said nothing,
patted his wife's cheek.

At his bedside, with brandy snifter,
he digests the molten encounter.
Recalls her breast brushing him,
inciting hot spring activity

He hungered to touch her,
chew her glazed lips,
dine on her rib.
Sip her.

In private dreams she feeds him.
But without real flesh,
nothing satisfies,
leaves him with a question.
Could fifty years of loyalty
be cancelled like a dinner reservation?

August Say Goodbye

August, say goodbye to them.
Watch her lover flee at dawn
down the dewy mountain moor
to the life to which he's sworn.

The stars' silhouette fading,
so too, the kisses on her lips
he bestowed as God does rain.
On her skin they turned to mist.

She captured his devotion,
her hazel gaze transcendent.
The quiet life she led,
reversed with her surrender.

As a flower to the sun
will evoke itself beyond
the boundary known as beauty,
just when summer's gone.

August, heed your salient end.
Your pretense, green to start,
her lover never will return,
false love proffered; he played the part.

A Man with a Bouquet

Both hands hold the stems
chosen with stampeding pulse.
Observe his gait, his smile.
Notice the neatness of his shirt,
the shine of his buckle,
socks snug around his ankles.

He must climb a staircase
to reach her front door.
Her nest awaits him.
He swims in her still gaze,
satin sheets and simple talk.

The current grows turbulent.
Passion wrestles with his reason.
Her fragrance admits to love.
Unknown to them, bouquets wither.

A Man who Makes Money

Can call me honey
it's quite all right
if his urge to merge
is just one night
I'll scramble his eggs
then his thoughts
he'll forget every ought
he ever was taught
I'll scrub his back
then turn around
let him poke me
to the ground
I'll shave his whiskers
on Saturday night
wrap my legs
around him tight
he'll own my flesh
I'll spend his cash
people will think
we found love at last
his horse comes in
his pockets are bulging
heads are turning
I'm the one he's holding

Some Things We're Forgetting

I'm forgetting to kiss you good night,
to button down your collar
to sew that hole in your sock.
But, that I love you, is certain.

You've forgotten to hold me at night,
to press your tongue against mine,
to look at me from across the room.
But, that you love me, is certain.

I make dinner, you take out the trash.
We change the sheets on Sunday,
stock up frequently on bounty and Charmin

That we love each other, is certain.
Do you remember falling in love?
I think I do. But I'm not certain.

SECTION TWO

NUCLEAR FAMILY

She Cannot Hear Me

The room is dark.
My mother is a mound in her bed.
At this threshold, I do not dare to speak.
I stay quiet to prevent her waking.
When she wakes, I will not tell her
what my children tell me.
They tell me I am cruel.
I search for their truth.
I cannot find it.
I know I am un-gentle.
I know it came from her.
I believe she loved the way she could.
I believe my children will know I did too.

When she lets go,
I will change the sheets,
sanitize the despair,
make orderly my thoughts,
plump the pillows
to soften the past,
then greet the guests.

Ink-Blot Memories of My Mother

Breath, quiet as a cat's paw,
your life slinks away.
Parched tongue in your open mouth,
I never heard you speechless.

I take your hand, fleshy and warm.
Images sway like bamboo in strong wind.
I choke back black ink.
The sound I make is soft, like a cat's purr.
The wind dies down. The bamboo straightens.

Time to remove my shield, rest my sword;
they failed to protect me anyway.
Will take to my grave the dread
I glued to the judicious way you loved.
No sense now to decry you. Better just to cry.

I scrub the sink with fervor to reshape
ink-blot memories of us into a still-life.
My arms are wrapped around you.
My cheek and yours touch.
We are both speechless.

See how the cat sits in your lap.

Gloria's Last Crossword Puzzle

Was still on the kitchen table.
115 across, "move like a peacock"…strut
108 down, "wrath"…ire
60 down, "give up"…not yet filled in…she did
"I'm done"
Three one-hundred-hour morphine drip bags.
12 days.

This was different.
Not fixable like the pearls
that needed restringing.
Not just a moment's squeeze
on the shoehorn.
The ceaseless debate about how much coffee
is too much coffee, was over.

Of breath, coffee, pearls,
crosswords swollen feet,
at 95, she preferred the open spaces

I stare
at so many unanswered clues.
The mystery of her.

My Mother Always Fed the Birds

I sit with coffee in the predawn dark,
remember your outstretched arms,
your hands dipping into seed for hungry birds

A full moon touches the winter solstice,
softens my cold memories of you.
I was hungry too.

I want to safekeep you
in a place we found
bread and laughter,
like at our kitchen table.

To store my love for you,
I search for when we last held hands.
Do wings mean birds don't drown?

My Mother's Magnifying Mirror

I always wanted my mother's magnifying mirror.
When she died, I took it.
Now that mirror is mine.
Then why is she still in there?
Her yellowing teeth, her splotches.

That blackhead on her left cheekbone,
like a doorbell, always there
when I drove her somewhere.
Her lipstick creeping into outcropped creases
on her upper lip.

She dictated driving instructions.
Never apologized for wrong addresses,
for the 3.2 miles out of our way,
the 3.2 miles back,
on the Los Angeles freeway.

That front seat magnified everything.
I use lip-liner, but I know, and she knew,
I share her destination.
My lipstick creeps into my upper
and my lower lip.

Momma Can't Answer

310-476-0128
Don't bother, it's disconnected now.
So is Mom.
I dialed every night for 10 years after Lou died.
There was little new news.
Sometimes she didn't answer,
always watching Turner classic movies.
I regret not buying her a sound bar.

I have the spaghetti colander from Matlock Street.
Took it 52 years ago,
moved a dozen times since then.
Will never leave it behind,
or the wooden cutting board.
Not memories, just reminders.
I had a childhood.

Then again,
I can hear a sizzling,
see her hand on her hip,
long fork flipping the bacon,
yellow scrambled eggs,
scratch of butter on toast,
the 1950s percolator.

Sunday's memory, like a found claim check.
The rest, forced through ducts
like the fry smoke sucked out the kitchen vent.

She Doesn't Even Know

My husband prays.
I hear his hushed shuffle,
three ritual steps forward, three back.
He is praying for my mother
on the third anniversary of her death.

He is the one who lights the *yahrzeit* candle,
a small tin cup which protects the flame.
Memories of her flicker.
I take another sip of my beer.

She assigned her body to science.
Positive for covid,
it never left her death-bed gurney.

He stopped the cremation
to protect her Jewish soul.
She doesn't know
we will be buried next to her.
She doesn't even know she is buried.

Rush

My mother has died.
She has not said a word since then.
The cicadas speak this year
after seventeen years underground.

She needed to rest
from the pain, from the pain killers.
She wanted to be dead.

Her decision,
she rushed to start the morphine drip,
didn't wait until I arrived.

The spotlight on the Chinese armoire
casts a small glow on her painting above.
I pretend she will emerge from the pagodas
she has hidden behind the trees.

I stand there to thank her from time to time,
ask her to explain why her name
is painted upside down at the top of her painting.

Who's your Daddy?

Not like dingy jazz lounge daddies
who teased with a single rose,
cajoled with chocolate covered strawberries,
wore aftershave strong as whiskey,
stashed bootleg under the bed.

Not like sugar-daddies who sent limos,
kissed my neck to get a whiff,
showed me off to their poker friends
who fought to light my cig.
Swore they'd leave their wives.

But, rather, who's *my* Daddy?
Oh, handsome father of vapors,
magicians disappear, then reappear.
Not you, Poof!
Stranded in the suburbs in the fifties,
I waited for you, for a father
like the fathers who locked the house,
turned out the lights promised safe sleep.

I prowled until I found a man
who would *be* Father to my children,
not just of them.

I still expect you to appear.
Even if it is your ghost,
I would recognize you.

I buried you but won't visit your grave
Gone too, is my need to hear you say you're sorry.

168th and Broadway

A man on 168th St. in New York City
sold me three T-shirts for ten dollars.
They came from China.
How was it possible to grow the cotton
pick it, truck it to the factory
weave into T-shirts,
sail them to America,
sell me three for ten dollars?
So the man could pay for groceries
walk home, cook dinner?

I was on 168th St.
to visit my son in a psychiatric ward
at Columbia Presbyterian Hospital.
The next time I was on 168th St.
he was selling lipstick.
Designer name for five dollars.
I had purchased this lipstick downtown for fifty
cursing myself every time I used it.
But here I was on 168th St.
and the lipstick was five dollars.
I could get used to this.

My son was committed for twenty-one days
That is how I found out he is bipolar.
I took the D train from midtown Manhattan
every night to visit. One night, just before
I started down the subway steps,
I felt a little chip.
It was a piece of my front tooth.
It fell onto my tongue.

Double Doors

There are double doors to get into the psych ward.
We remove all portable objects.
One door closes and locks behind us.
Another one buzzes open.
We enter with nothing.

Here, a day is a week, is a month,
all measureless intervals for reckoning.
All crawling.

We know how bones knit,
but not how the mind mends.
He spins delusions as if with a crochet hook.
A mother's hand on a forehead does no good.

We sift and calculate for reasons.
We nod, we love, we want.
We want, we want, we want to undo this.
What we want does not matter.

We gather our portable objects.
Both doors close, lock behind us.
We leave with nothing.

For my son

There is no metaphor. He was thirty-four.
Bipolar.
Agony mixed with hope:
stupefied us through the shock of the first episode,
stymied us at the surprise of the second,
permitted us to accept the diagnosis at the third,
crawled us out of the fourth.
We are in the fifth.

If only these were innings, this a baseball game.
I'm rooting hard for my son.
I believe he'll hit a homer with bases loaded,
become the champion I know he is.

You son, you must grip the bat,
hold your feet on the ground, solid, determined,
swing like your life depended on it.
It does; as does ours.
Send the demon out of the park.

I see you on a victory run heading for home plate.

Make Believe

Long ago I brushed her hair.
The tickle made her giggle
when she curtseyed to greet our guests.
They clapped their hands, looked my way.
Believing she was my accomplishment,
I reveled in their admiration.

We wove flower tiaras,
make-believe futures.
Daisy-crowns stained her pillow.
I scrubbed it clean and plumped it.
Her pulse, my purpose,
we romped from room to room.
She never needed no-more-tears shampoo.

I didn't know she kept coiled secrets
inside those childhood curls.
I cannot comb out the knots.
I try, but cannot enter the tunnel
she channeled to her womanhood.
Nightmares stain her pillow now.

If I could take her back to then
I would bathe her again in make-believe
until she could believe make-believe is real.

Polyester Never Dies

These sheets wrapped my children's dreams.
Pink and yellow ruffles under chins,
stars warded off the boogeyman.
They've been moved three times to second homes.
Now, they share summer closet shelves
with dormant daddy long-legs.

In dim light on this gray wet day,
I rub my hand over them.
Attempt to ignite the crackle of static-cling,
to jolt back to young motherhood
when my legs were climbing-trees,
my arms, swings,
my chest, their pillow.
With flashlights under sheet tents,
we landed on the moon.

I will make them crackle again.
These sheets wait for their children
to take their first moonwalk with me.
Wrinkle free, permanent-press, unlike me.

Daddy long-legs awakens,
strides over my still hand,
slips under a fold.
I wonder how old he is.
If, like polyester, he will never die?
If I'm not here, tell your children
your mother taught you how to fly.

SECTION THREE

REFLECTIONS

Stingy

His sign said "hungry".
I gave him just one dollar.
Could have given five.
but I won't tell you,
he was missing both his legs.
I wouldn't miss the five,

His Cart

He has wheels on his shopping cart
to cart his life.
Black plastic bags, cast like buoys,
bulge with possessions
to claim his roots in homelessness.

My Lexus has wheels. The trunk always full
with the same black plastic bags
I cart from, not one, but two homes.

I spotted him in Riverside Park at a forked path.
I thought about the choice he once made.
Was it his choice?

I could not take my eyes off him.
The color of skin,
neglect, terror, hunger, snow, rain,
the brutal winds on the Hudson River.
I shivered.

I had coffee in bed this morning,
the sun sparking the river for my amusement.
My double paned windows, my doormen
protect my protected life.

Both of us standing still. Was he looking at me,
the way I was looking at him?
Was he also wondering about fairness?
Life, an empty cart,
ours to fill.

On My Walk

When I reach the old wooden bulwark,
I stop and wait until I know why I have stopped.
Worn, but still standing, come-upon old age,
survived Gardiners Bay white-capped winter blasts.
Jagged grey peaks measure what is missing
as if to remind the passer-by that we'll go missing.

Don't know who or why
they took down the fishing nets.
I miss the bearded seamen
scudding in their small skiffs,
the smell of steaming coffee,
our morning hello waves.
Their deep rutted faces showed me nothing
was missing from their lives.

I hired Arturo to dig a garden for me.
He sings and whistles to himself.
His face is also rutted.
I stop and wait until I know why I listen.

It is this weathering of men
who trust the earth or the sea
to make them whole.

I collect empty conch shells,
even just spiral remnants.
They don't have to be whole

Do Not Do

Replaced with delinquent purpose,
I'm done with necessary doing.

A pebble accepts my aimless kicks,
on a zig-zag walk to the beach.
I usually front the wind with my face,
to earn an easy return.
Today, the wind is my sail on the outward bound,
the consequence, an arduous return.
I will welcome the fatigue,
an invitation to sit in the sand, do nothing.

On my way home,
my pebble encourages me to kick harder,
for a longer zig-zag joy ride.

I cut the bottoms off my bell-bottoms,
didn't hem them. Let the fringe begin!

Things

There were so many things:
porcelain, crystal, stainless steel,
wide neck vases for roses,
globe shaped for tulips,
a slender bud vase for single stems.

Not to mention all the teeth, the grins, the cheers,
embraces from all the limbs on two family trees.
Hugs and pats…congrats!

Fifth floor walk-up,
there was no place to stuff the stuff.
Eventually, an elevator, a foyer, a kitchen window
All things found a place worthy of their sentiment.

Breakage…one by one…year by year,
as each thing disappeared.
Indoor games of hide and seek,
flailing arms and running feet.
Would have traded all those things
for a washing machine.

Then came a cavernous home,
ill-timed, at the time of preferring less,
there would be less to shed.
The backwards fate of things and space
assuming acquisition claimed assurance.

Time now to donate all the rest,
except the slender bud vase.
Its purpose so precise,
taking up such little space.

Evening Fire

Orange riot, boogie-woogie-peek-a-boo,
ignoring the contradiction of its fate,
willing to die, resurrect, die again,
martyr to heat my bones.

This was my tree.
Shared shade, spread limbs for birds,
bore fruit, hoisted children to its swing,
gave and gave again.

I watch this once stalwart friend
burn in my blackened fireplace. Death's portal.
Tomorrow, I will sweep its quiet ash,
silken to the touch, reminded of impermanence.

When I am disassembled, will I feel like silk?
Did I provide sufficient refuge for those I loved?
To live another winter day is plum.
The carbon of us all.

At Quail Hill Farm

Farm girls astride tractors,
thick rubber treads emboss ruddy soil.
They ride their thrones with certainty.

Dirt under their nails,
emblems of Earth-queens,
rugged female farmers.

Hoes in hand, summer glazed faces.
A pose beguiling as the curve of lips
in Mona Lisa's smile.

Farm girls seeding in seductive loam
glimpse a private splendor
when hand buries seed.
Both creator and created,
the tossed stone and its ripple.

Moss

Moss quietly quilts the earth
gathers tightly
yet does not lay down roots
does not succumb to wind
requires no affection
will not drown by flood
will not starve by drought
it needs no height to stand
nor sun to thrive
does not demand a hill
softens edges of rocks
makes love with tree-bark
Invites rain under its skin
whispers good night to the worms
allows the feet of children to play
or the feet of men march to war

Just Pretendin'

He wasn't doing anything he wasn't supposed to.
Just mowing the lawn as always,
gawking sideways at the convertible on the driveway,
trying not to stare at the pink girl in the front seat,
trying not to listen to her giggling on the phone.

Just trim a little longer in that spot, that's all.
No harm, try not to be noticed,
head down pretending he needed to crank his motor.

This girl always forgets something.
She runs back to the house
with those red painted toes
He whiffs her perfume. He was that close.

He's going 100 miles per hour,
wherever he wants and she's going with him.
They're cruising, his channel on the radio.
She's smiling.
Always respectful, just pretending.

Three Clocks

One says 10:27.
I must have already had dinner.
one says 8:27.
I must be very hungry.
One says 5:27.
I wonder what is for dinner.

Ask me what I eat.
I eat my appetite,
the thing that craves, lusts, devours.

Let's Schmooz

It's time to take my time.
Get off this bullet-train,
"How are you?"
My figure-eight response,
"Fine, how are you?"
Time to pull the emergency brake.

Time to stop double-thinking conversations,
measuring, assessing, calculating
who lands on top. Utilitarian, yes.
So many syllables. I'm exhausted.

I love popcorn.
Saturday night, big home screen, butter.
Finger-lickin' simple talk,
guess who did it.
Feels good to share small stuff.

Eight, sideways, is infinity:
a bow, a butterfly,
A friendship.

I like my coffee black.
Let us go sideways.
Let's schmooze.

His Grandpa's Tree

His father waited
until he was certain of his own death
to tell his son tales of this tree.

His grandpa and the sapling were the same height
when he carved his initials with his first knife.
Sap oozed like blood from the lime green inner skin.
It healed. They became best friends.
He didn't cry when he stubbed his toe on a root.
His to climb, to dream.

The trunk grew so large,
no one at Sunday barbecue noticed
when grandpa kissed grandma for the first time.
Her wedding garland woven with silver-tipped spring leaves.
Picnics with their children on land they owned.
Old age unfurled under straw hats, their hands clasped.

One more tale to tell.
His father drove him one hundred miles
to see the branch
used to lynch his grandpa when they took his land.

His grandon bought the land, cut down the tree.
The black log lingers in the fireplace;
a barely noticeable draft kindles
the funeral pyre remnant.

The tree does not remember his grandpa.
The tree does not remember itself.

A Gift from Bob

I lost the key chain Bob made for me fifty years ago.
Bob fled to Canada during the Vietnam war.
I was a lifer in graduate school.
We both wore long hair, fringed bleached bell bottoms.
Our hippie culture made it easy to be just friends.

A circle, like all the letters in his name,
it was hand-tooled etched leather,
the color of western brown cowboy boots.
It made me feel rugged, close to the earth, safe.
That key chain had exclusive rights to my palm.

The key chain never wore out,
 like the stepping-stone in a river
 that lets you know you can cross.

I lost Bob's gift two years ago on a rainy day.
My coat pockets worn out from searches,
countless riffling reveals nothing
but tissues, candy wrappers, coins.
Tiny tantrums, moderate curses, fail.

With each search, I whisper out loud,
"They only went to sleep."

Just after he gave me this gift,
Bob and his wife died in their van
on a camping trip from carbon monoxide.

The Nurse

She touched my arm, said my name.
I was hers, learned her name,
rehearsed it, so I could thank her.
Farro was her name.
Farro from the Philippines,
in her blue scrubs, squeaky shoes, mask.
The machine went round and round,
the dye inserted for contrast.
She touched my arm again,
called me by my name again.
"Thank you, Farro."
Her cheeks smiled under her mask.
Finally, a sip of coffee.
Later that day I thought of her,
the splendid roundness of her face.
Farro, the Filipino nurse.

Bus Route out my Window during Covid

From the 15th floor I see the numbers
on the hydroelectric buses on Riverside Drive.
I see the same bus numbers every day
This is their route.
No one gets off. No one gets on.
They stop at red lights.

I think this is a waste of money.
Then I think
what if
one bus driver
picks up one nurse
who saves one life.

No Ordinary Lemon

My friend gave me a small lemon he picked in Israel.
I found it weeks later in my refrigerator.
Tinged green, shrunken, I thought to throw it out.

Shabbos approaching, burners flaming,
my kitchen counters cluttered.
Feast day on my side of the world,
removed from the war in Israel.

Curious, I sliced the puny Israeli lemon.
Razor thin skin offered no resistance.
I squeezed its flesh.
My wet fingers dredged for pits.
Its plentiful juice a sweet sour,
its color, the softness of the sun.
An oasis. It did not make sense.

This was no ordinary lemon.
I saw the destroyed kitchens in Israel.
My *Shabbos* safe, I sliced it without fear.

My Prayer

How have you done all this?
Your lavender is my heartbeat,
your green the energy of my soul.
I would exchange my fingerprints
for the bark on a cherry tree
I am lucky.
I don't need to adhere to scripture
to embrace your eternity,
only to bend my knee, touch your ground.
My devotion is immediate.
I do not get tired or hungry
I am yours for the taking.
Touch is our manifestation.
I know that you are here,
that we have met.

Zen in Hand… Haiku Gusts

If you are not dead
you can still claim victory
over circumstance

Pandemic moment
thieves stole the toilet paper
left the jewels here

My pen is my Zen
you cannot hook me by words
I am not a fish

I find a feather
the bird wants me to have it
left here just for me

Prune the trees this year
sometimes too much is too
much prune your life now too

Socks you hate to wear
yes, that particular pair
throw them out today

The birds owe me song
two times each day I feed them
is poop gratitude

This sky is pale white
a good day for soft white thoughts
the air is so still.

I am not a bird
I must make big decisions
 beyond limbs of trees

I am not a bird.
big choices beyond tree limbs
yes, I can soar too

Thoughts ought to be fought
Not all, just the ones that hurt
others need your love

Summer day darkened
I decided to love you
then daylight returned

Arturo digs ditch
sings and whistles to himself
jealous, I watch him

She tilts on a breeze
wispy geisha girl daydreams
a chive strokes her cheek

This spring is now here
no longer waiting for it
what to do with it

Strange purple feathers
arrive in my nighttime dreams
bring fanciful flight

Butter and sea salt
the birds won't eat my popcorn
they're smarter than me

Four Haiku about Birds

I rise to curse them
blackened harmonies goad me
unconstrained contempt

Instead, I feed them
they eat in silence
I think I'm owed melody

Caws, sideways glances
they do not sing for my joy
they are not my friends

my warm bed still waits
not contempt, indifference,
debt-free they escape

Sea Between us

Two birds are in love
feed each other sure footed
in public no less

We were copycats
fed by the arc of four wings
drifted in curled waves

Something cold happened
summer grasshopper is dead
green sea flattened out

My skin is peeling
locked suitcase sits near a door
dark sea between us

SECTION FOUR

ANIMALS OF ANY KIND

Migration

For one night they've come to my willowed marsh
to rest in the autumn dark beneath a slim moon.
Their melody guides me past summer's green
to a path I've not been on before.

I arrive at their survival route, lie at the rim of their circle,
wait until my thoughts no longer govern me.
Then, with an outstretched hand
that wants not to be afraid, dare to caress them.
They don't startle. Their breath is warm.

I've entered their hushed serenity
on pillows of breathing feathered breasts.
I move closer to their heartbeats,
to disrupt the drumbeat of my thoughts.

I eavesdrop on giddy gaggled conversations.
They praise their young for keeping up.
The marsh, so comfortable,
they may stay another night.
Surprised, we understand each other,
I say, "oh please do."
They settle into sleep. The crickets too.

They stayed another night as they said they would.
Left me with an ache
on this path I've not been on before.
I'd like to know where I'm going without GPS.
I want to die on Earth's crust without fear.

In the beak of Prayer

The falcon's talon tightens on its prey.
His sweeping grace, tunneled aim, temerity, timing
beg me to forgive his tyranny.
His chain of cunning leaves no doubt or leftovers.
A form of G-d's attendant perfection,
catch or be caught in binary certitude.

I pray,
believing a chain of devotion will leave no doubts,
sequenced strands of grace will be left over.
Another form of G-d's ordained perfection.

We both hunt with perfect clutch, whether for flesh or faith.

In my Pool

An old fly, a young cricket
rolled as if they were following me.
The pool boy will vacuum them, alive or dead.

I thought of decaying would-be immigrants
at the bottom of those exotic vacation seas,
the Mediterranean, the Aegean, the Caribbean,
capsized, rolling with determined open eyes.

88 degrees, half-naked, speedo cap and goggles,
I turn my cheek every other stroke,
try to forgive myself for staying afloat.

Send his Body Home

Perched on a rib cage,
drenched by the soldier's wound,
a vulture's wings are blood-tipped.
Eyes, sentries, guard the kill
he knows he has not earned.
Even so, his loud caw proclaims victory.

The soldier's mother prays daily,
but doubt invades.
Now she must beg G-d.

His wife speaks of him as she feeds their son.
His slippers warm her.
She re-irons his shirts,
searches for hints she can smell.

A mother, a child, a wife, a soldier, a bird, a war.
Shifting positions, claws slip deeper into the dead.

Today I'll Stay Still

This humidity is silk.
Keep it on my skin please.
No need to think past my breath.

I'll stay still, as the deer in the wood,
listens for an inkling sound
with only a twitch of her ear,
but does not dart.

Not a muscle of mine will move.
A slow turtle can get run over.
A speeding car can swerve.
What are my chances?

It's good to be slow sometimes.
Today, I'm not in a hurry.
Neither are the bees
who, like me, work for a living.

If the phone rings, I won't answer.
I'm not here now.
I'm with that deer
watching a bee nap on a stamen.

The Steer

Never warned,
he will be lassoed,
hooves quadrupled in ropes,
thrown to the ground.
Foamed saliva, short snorts,
a wild eye on the leather cowboy boot
trespassing on his neck.

He doesn't know he's in a rodeo.
There, to pulse a crowd.
He wants his mother.
He will not find her again.

Men with guns and spurs,
raised on extreme excitement,
taught to witness suffering,
to impose it, then swagger,
own the final say.
They raise their hats,
squint into the sun,
say, "We win."

A Stallion in my Dream

Up before the songbirds, I stare at the bird feeder
rub a cuticle.
The sliding door creaks, the snow caves
as I pour no-waste bird food from the holiday tin.
A waft of peanuts floats.
Today the sun hides,
low tide sucks the trapped foot of a swan.
Day breaks, the birds still sleep.
Expecting a genie, I keep rubbing.

Last night in my dream, a stampeding stallion
mocked the distance and my pace
from my back door to the birdfeeder.
I mounted bareback, my cheek on his neck.
I snorted, "don't you see Mt Everest!"
Did I imagine climbing all those peaks?
There was only dust on my trail.
Red digital time galloped.

The birds are awake.
I need to hear them sing.
I open the heavy sliding door.
Invite winter in.

I Thought I had a bad night

Until I saw an ant climbing my toilet wall.
Thought of Sisyphus and Jewish slaves.
Halfway up he would fall,
then start again with no revision of his route.
I considered, only briefly, a flush.
Scooped him in a crumpled tissue, not to crush.
It's April, I justified,
he could live outside with relatives.
But it's early April, mornings 29 degrees.
Drenched, exhausted, he might freeze.
I am no executioner! He slipped out.
Loose tissues are defective transports.
Next time, an all-terrain vehicle.
With gusto he fled across the bathroom floor.
A bulbous hardy lad with prehistoric features,
he'll make a good father.
He must be hungry.
I ran to fetch a sugar cube.
By my return, he was gone.
Popped the cube in my mouth.

Swansong

One of the swans has died.
The lone one swims in silence as they both did.
Entwined by their rippled circles,
their silence didn't sound like silence,
didn't feel like loneliness.

Deep on dark green Gardiners Bay,
weathered pilings framed their stage.
Still shoals surrounded their quiet ballet.
Terns scooted me to a stony seat.
Gulls pulled back the cloud curtains.

In spring their cygnets trailed them.
Swirly bumper-swans formed a Fosse chorus line.
By fall, all but the Mr. and Mrs. left town.

This winter there is only one.
I say how sorry I am for you.
This lonely one won't look my way.
I take my front row seat for his swansong.

Hoarder

Sunless day in October,
a dove pecks, the jay squawks.
The chipmunk stuffs his cheeks.

Not cold, not hot, so temperate
I forget the summer struggle
to move deep-rooted trees,
navigate the shifting sun,
outwit invasive growth,
control color schemes.

Devoured by my frenzy for beauty.
like me, the chipmunk does not stop to eat.
Stores more and more.

I admire this passionate hoarder.
He will not starve this winter.
Nor will I.

Uterine Traveler

Migrating from a purple ovary,
trailblazing beyond passion
in a small, yet limitless, space,
I somersault.

There are no toothaches; I'm never hungry.
This dark try-on room for souls is safe.
Let me imbibe the saline nutrients
in this tumbling, swimmable murk.
A mitosis-wind is at my back.

My first thoughts are of freedom.
My feet want to touch the ground.
Tell me I'm not dreaming
when I'm born in America.

I could be someone,
own a house one day,
train a horse to ride in rodeo,
save a mouse from drowning.

Crabgrass

I welcome this sturdier broadleaf,
stiffer than the Kentucky-blue, red-fescue mix.
It's hardy and just as green as the luxury blend
which loses the perennial mid-summer battle.
However, it does suffocate the bouncy sprigs of clover
preferred by the rabbit who appears nightly,
until the crabgrass invades.

He goes south of the highway,
to the lacy lawns behind the hedges
where crabgrass is banned.

I will miss his cottontail, quiet munch,
his perfunctory rejection of my evening carrot.
But, tonight he shares my carrot,
the tell-tale sign he'll be on his way.

Camouflage

A whippoorwill from my wooded garden
followed me to New York city.
When I opened my high-rise apartment window,
I heard him say,
"It's time to leave this city.
Your grey wool suits, woven with steel nerves, have frayed.
Your rhythm in high heels is off.
You no longer need to match sweaters
with chameleon lips.
The homeless shake dirty plastic cups for change.
It's time for you to change.
I live in a tree in your garden.
See how my feathers match the bark.
No hawk can find me.
Come live with me."
I closed my window. He flew from my ledge.
My fingers turned to vines.

The Mosquito Bite
…a tribute to Sun Tzu's Art of War

I have coated my skin with citronella,
lit the cedarwood incense.
The anti-mosquito sound machine is on.
The blue light is within 20 feet of the table.

I could
spare the blood,
dismiss the sting,
endure the itch.

All he wants is a pinch, to stay alive.
What the mosquito really wants,
is what I want from you.

Please Come Out

On this smooth, silver platinum August night
the sway of the black locust tree
touches the rims of the clouds.

Please come out.
Drink wine with me and listen.
Listen to nothing else, nothing else.

I promise you,
If you hear a mosquito,
see a mosquito,
feel a mosquito,
we'll run inside.

Just this once,
please come out.
Listen to this night.

2:32 AM

Stillness on this page.
The fly not flying,
like me, not sleeping.

He crawls on my words.
Neither of us blink.
He pulls me somewhere.

Veined wing illumined by a full moon,
We watch each other.
He rubs himself.

We share the stillness,
the silence,
the full moon.

Both of us hungry,
he feeds me.
In return, I let him live.

Dee Slavutin has written two full length poetry collections: *Wingspan: Search for Food* and *Suddenly Deciduous*, which will be published in 2025 by Finishing Line Press. Dee has a Master's degree in Literature (McGill University) and an MBA in Finance (Fordham University). At McGill, Dee founded Cyan Line, a poetry magazine and served as its editor while completing her degree. She was a 2024 grant recipient from the Ruth Wisse Foundation as a finalist for her poem "Aging in Haiku." She curated the East Hampton Poetry Marathon for five years, a summer series of poetry readings. She was the president of a boutique financial services company for thirty plus years. Dee lives in East Hampton and New York City with her husband Lee. They have two grown children.

"I take long walks on Gardiner's Bay, the Atlantic Ocean, or in Riverside Park where poems are always formulating. Then, with pencil, I scratch, peck, plant, mend, write and rewrite until the story is told. I love the brevity of poetry, the fluidity and the completeness of the message." In the book My Name is Asher Lev, Chaim Potok's character says ...that additional aching surge of effort that is always the difference between integrity and deceit in a created work."

Contact: deeslavutin@gmail.com 917-319-1229

www.ingramcontent.com/pod-product-compliance
Lightning Source LLC
Chambersburg PA
CBHW030054170426
43197CB00010B/1521